What Do ASTRONAUTS Do?

I LIKE SPACE!

Carmen Bredeson

WORDS TO KNOW

engineering (en jih NEER ing)
The study of how things work.

laboratory (LA bruh tor ee)
A place for testing things.

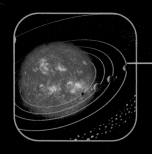

orbit (OR bit)
To go around something.

CONTENTS

What is an astronaut?

Men and women who work in space are called astronauts. Some are pilots who fly spaceships. Others study things in a laboratory. Each person has a job to do during a trip to space.

What is it like to blast into space?

Astronauts strap into their seats. Rocket engines *ROAR!* The spaceship starts to shake as it lifts off. UP it goes! About eight minutes later the ship starts to orbit Earth.

Fun Fact

Astronauts wear diapers during liftoff. They may be strapped into their seats for many hours before the spaceship blasts off.

This space shuttle is lifting off.

What is it like to be in space?

Everything floats! Astronauts do not walk. They float around the spaceship. Some look out the windows at the beautiful Earth. The ship goes all the way around Earth every hour and a half.

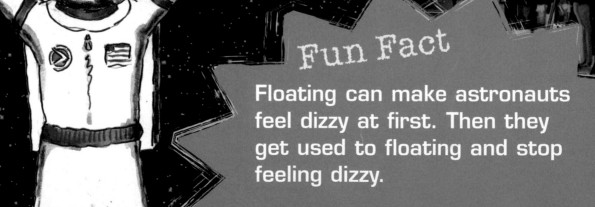

Fun Fact

Floating can make astronauts feel dizzy at first. Then they get used to floating and stop feeling dizzy.

What is the space station?

The space station is a big laboratory. It moves in orbit high above Earth. Scientists live there to study how objects act in space. They even study how *they* act in space!

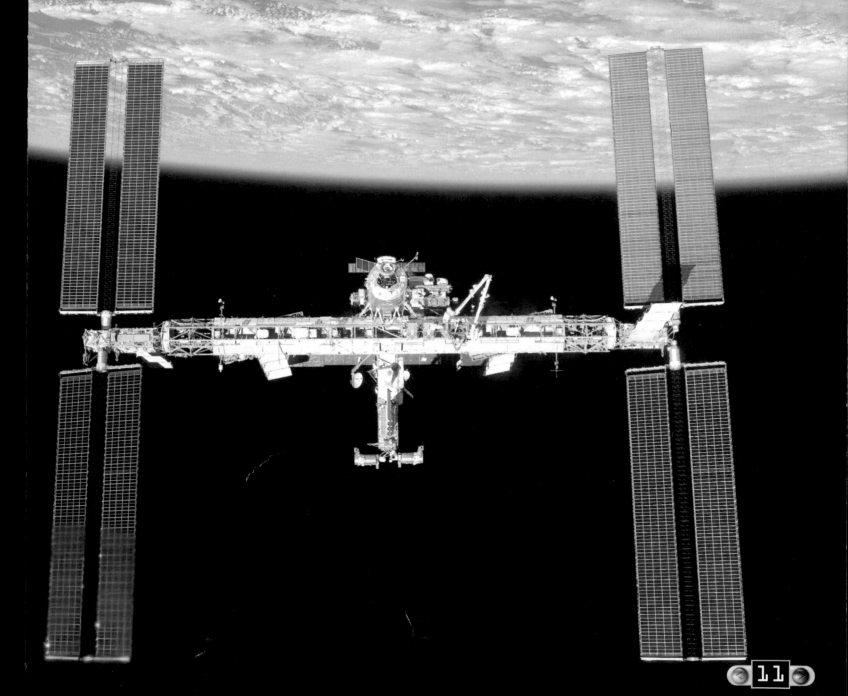

What do astronauts do in space?

Astronauts study how things grow in space.
They also test machines that will be used on
trips to the Moon or Mars.
Some astronauts take space walks.
Others study whether people can stay
healthy in space.

Fun Fact

There is no up or down in
space. The floor and walls
seem just the same as the
ceiling.

HATC

What are space walks?

Sometimes astronauts need to go outside the spaceship or space station to work. Then they wear big space suits. The suits protect them from hot and cold temperatures. The suits also give them air to breathe.

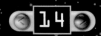

What do astronauts eat in space?

Astronauts eat food that is cooked on Earth and put into bags. Turkey, nuts, tortillas, shrimp, and yogurt are some things an astronaut eats in space.

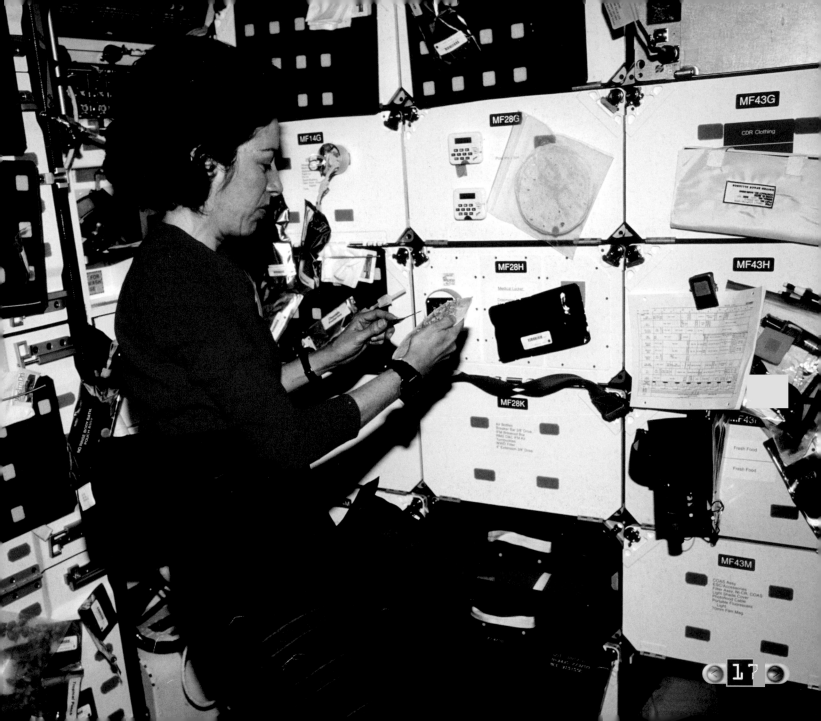

How do astronauts stay clean in space?

There are no showers on spaceships.
Water floats away. Astronauts use wet towels
and hand wipes to stay clean.
Toothpaste sticks to toothbrushes.
Astronauts can brush their teeth upside down!

Fun Fact

Astronauts cannot spit
toothpaste into a sink. The
toothpaste is a special kind
that they can swallow. They
can also spit it into a tissue.

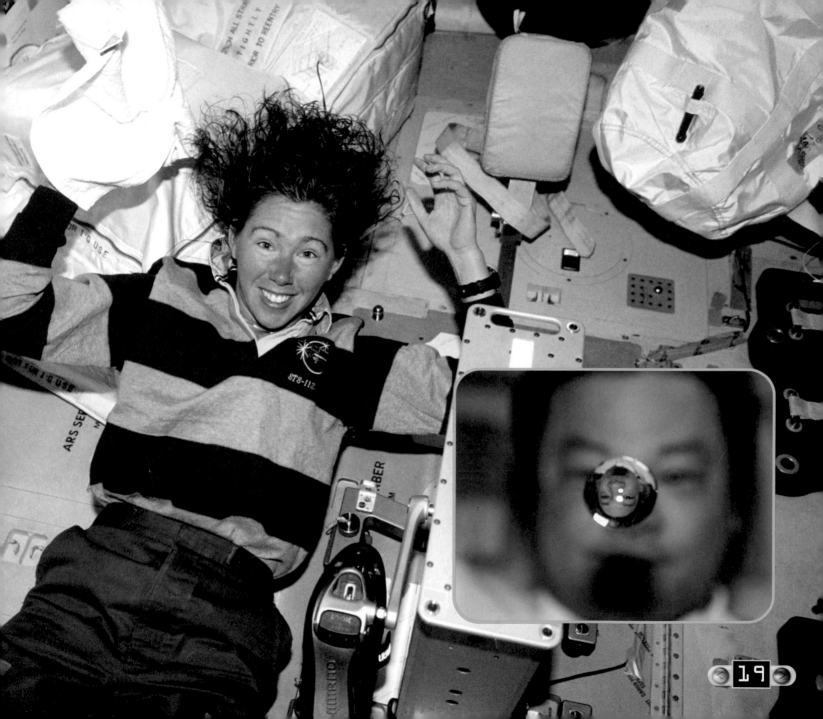

How do astronauts go to the bathroom?

There is a toilet on the spaceship. An astronaut uses a belt and toe straps to stay down on the seat. Waste is sucked into a tank because EVERYTHING floats in space!

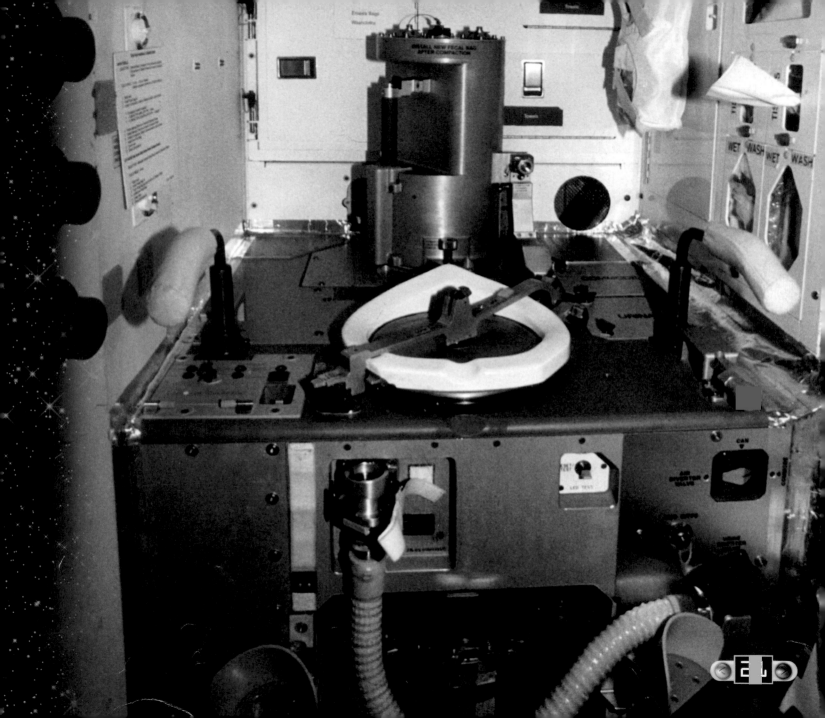

Why do astronauts exercise in space?

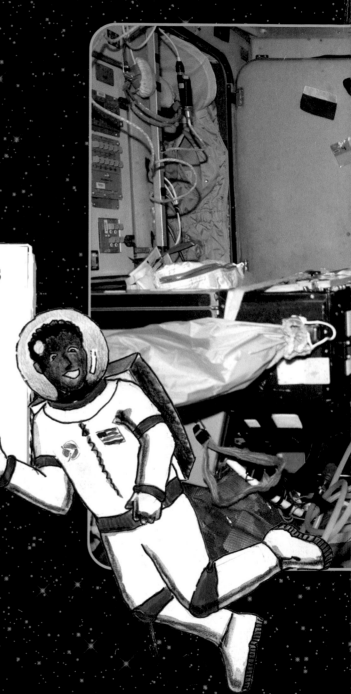

Floating does not use as many muscles as walking. Astronauts exercise every day to keep their bodies strong. Running on a treadmill is good exercise. Astronauts use straps to hold them down while they run.

treadmill

What do astronauts do for fun?

Doing flips in space is fun. So is playing with food. Astronauts toss juice blobs or candy. Then they try to catch them in their mouths. Some astronauts play musical instruments in space. They can even check their e-mail!

These astronauts eat gummy worms!

How do astronauts sleep?

Most astronauts use sleeping bags. The sleeping bags are attached to a wall or chair. Astronauts often wear a mask over their eyes to keep out the light. Some astronauts like to listen to music before they fall asleep.

Fun Fact

The youngest person to fly into space was Russian Gherman Titov. He was 25 years old when he flew in 1961. The oldest astronaut was John Glenn. He was 77 when he flew in 1998.

How does a person become an astronaut?

Astronauts must finish college. Most of them study math, science, computers, or engineering. Pilots are trained to fly jet planes. Astronauts also need to be very healthy. They exercise and eat good food to keep their bodies strong.

Floating in space is like floating underwater. Astronauts practice for a space walk in a swimming pool.

This astronaut uses a computer game to practice his job on the space station.

Some astronauts fly jet planes.

Would you like to be an astronaut?

Pilots fly spaceships.

Doctors take care of the crew in space.

Engineers keep the spaceships working.

Biologists and Chemists do experiments in space. They see how plants grow in space and how people feel in space.

Books

Adamson, Thomas K. *Astronauts*. Mankato, Minn.: Capstone Press, 2007.

Gibbons, Gail. *The Planets*. New York: Holiday House, 2005.

Shearer, Deborah A. *Astronauts at Work*. Mankato, Minn.: Bridgestone Books, 2002.

Web Sites

Living in Space
<http://spaceflight.nasa.gov/living/index.html>

NASA Space Place
<http://spaceplace.nasa.gov.en/kids/>

INDEX

To Kate, our shining star

Enslow Elementary, an imprint of Enslow Publishers, Inc.
Enslow Elementary® is a registered trademark of Enslow Publishers, Inc.

Library of Congress Cataloging-in-Publication Data

Bredeson, Carmen.
    What do astronauts do? / Carmen Bredeson.
        p. cm. — (I like space!)
    Summary: "Introduces early readers to subjects about space in Q&A format"—
Provided by publisher.
    Includes bibliographical references and index.
    ISBN-13: 978-0-7660-2942-2
    ISBN-10: 0-7660-2942-5
    1. Astronautics—Miscellanea—Juvenile literature. 2. Astronauts—Miscellanea—
Juvenile literature. I. Title.
    TL793.B7325 2008
    629.45-dc22   2007002742

Printed in the United States of America

10 9 8 7 6 5 4 3 2 1

To Our Readers: We have done our best to make sure all Internet Addresses in this book were
active and appropriate when we went to press. However, the author and the publisher have
no control over and assume no liability for the material available on those Internet sites or on
other Web sites they may link to. Any comments or suggestions can be sent by e-mail to
comments@enslow.com or to the address on the back cover.

Illustration Credits: Carl M. Feryok

Photo Credits: All photos courtesy of NASA, except as noted: Courtesy NASA/JPL-Caltech,
p. 2 (orbit); NASA/JAXA, p. 24; Shutterstock, blue starfield background and p. 2
(engineering).

Cover Photo:

Series Literacy Consultant:
Allan A. De Fina, Ph.D.
Past President of the New Jersey Reading Association
Chairperson, Department of Literacy Education
New Jersey City University, Jersey City, NJ

Series Science Consultant:
Marianne J. Dyson
Former NASA Flight Controller
Science Writer
www.mdyson.com

Enslow Elementary
an imprint of
Enslow Publishers, Inc.
40 Industrial Road
Box 398
Berkeley Heights, NJ 07922
USA
http://www.enslow.com